Spelling Helpline

A guide for parents, teachers, adults and
children with spelling difficulties

by

Jean Alston

Other titles by Dextral Books:

Writing Left-Handed
Handwriting Helpline
GCSEs: Surviving the Course
Write On Target
Left-Handed Helpline

Also by Jean Alston:

with Jane Taylor: Handwriting: Theory, Research and Practice, Routledge, London, 1987.

Writing Left-Handed, Left-Handed Company, Manchester, 1990, rev. 1991; reprinted Dextral Books, Manchester, 1992.

with Jane Taylor: Handwriting Helpline, Dextral Books, Manchester, 1990.

Assessing and Promoting Writing Skills, NASEN, Stafford, 1993.

All rights reserved. No part of this publication may be produced or transmitted in any form or by any means, electronic or mechanical, including photocopying, recording, or any information storage and retrieval system, without the prior permission in writing from the publishers. The illustrations on pages 16 and 18 may be photocopied for use by teachers free of charge.

British Library Cataloguing-in-Publication Data

A catalogue record for this book is
available from the British Library

*First published 1992. Revised 1994
by Dextral Books, PO Box 52, South DO, Manchester M20 2PJ.*

Copyright © 1992 by Jean Alson

ISBN *1 872177 07 7*

CONTENTS

		Page
Introduction		4
1.	The National Curriculum	5
2.	The Importance of Correct Spelling in Examinations	7
3.	Some Things to Remember	8
4.	Some Questions and Answers	9
5.	Visual Memory	10
6.	Auditory Memory	11
7.	Sound-to-Symbol Memory	12
8.	Words Needed Most for Spelling and Writing	13
9.	Key Words to Literacy	14
10.	Key Word Spelling Record	16
11.	Second Key Word Spelling Record	18
12.	Letters and Syllables	20
13.	Closed Syllables	21
14.	Open Syllables	22
15.	Vowel-Consonant-e Syllables	23
16.	Diphthong Syllables	24
17.	Consonant-l-e Syllables	25
18.	Syllables with Vowel-r	26
19.	Syllable Practice	27
20.	Developing Spelling through Meaning	28
21.	Tests	32
22.	Addresses and Information	34

Introduction

This booklet is for:

a) Parents who wish to help their children;
b) Older pupils who wish to find a method for improving their spelling;
c) Adults whose spelling remains at a reasonably basic level of success.

Many publications tell their readers **which** words they should learn to spell by providing little more than the very lists which have already confused those with spelling problems. If you want to overcome your spelling difficulties, the first step is to develop a technique for learning which will work for you. With this technique, the words to be learnt are less important, because you can apply the successful learning method to **all** the words you come across.

The National Curriculum is now of prime importance in our education, and parents reading this booklet will learn what is expected of their children in school.

Words used most often for reading and writing have been highlighted. At first sight, these Key Words seem quite simple, but they occur so often in writing, that it is essential that they should be spelt correctly. A special check list to help pupils to do this is provided.

Words are made up of letters, sounds and syllables and a section of the booklet is devoted to teaching the reader about them. People with dyslexic tendencies need to learn the mechanics of spelling, and they will find the special spelling techniques and the information about letters, sounds and syllables particularly useful. As well as knowing about letters, sounds and syllables, it is helpful to know word meanings, and to recognise that adding word beginnings (prefixes) and word endings (suffixes) will change the meaning of the words we write.

A test at the end of the booklet highlights words which may have to be relearnt. This can also be used before beginning, to work out which sections of the booklet need the most attention.

The National Curriculum

Q: **What does the National Curriculum require that my child should be taught?**

A: As the national Curriculum has changed during its consultation periods, it has gradually become more precise about the teaching of spelling. Although it would be impossible to refer to all teaching stages, the following major aspects of our spelling system are mentioned in detail. Your child should be instructed in the following manner.

Conventional spelling should be encouraged from the beginning. This will be brought about by a number of recommendations in the Programmes of Study:

Because handwriting and spelling go hand in hand, at an early stage, pupils should be taught to form lower case and capital letters correctly.

They should learn to write common letter strings within familiar and common words, for example, in their own name, and in words like 'ring', 'hand' and 'shop'. They should be able to remember these words so that they can write them correctly in their general writing. By the end of Key Stage One, they should be able to spell simple polysyllabic words, such as 'because, after, open, teacher, animal and together', correctly.

Towards the end of Key Stage One (7 year-olds), they should learn the terms 'vowel' and 'consonant'. They should begin to learn about prefixes and suffixes.

Prefixes are put at the beginnings of words, and change the meaning, so that:

inhabited	becomes	**UN**inhabited
hospitable	becomes	**IN**hospitable
legal	becomes	**IL**legal
relevant	becomes	**IR**relevant

Suffixes are put at the ends of words, change their meanings and make them into different parts of speech or grammar, so that:

comfort	becomes	comfort**ABLE**
happy	becomes	happi**NESS**
wonder	becomes	wonder**FUL**

At Key Stage Two of the National Curriculum, pupils should have and be aware of their own written word bank, i.e. a group of words that they can write correctly. They should use a dictionary to check the spelling and meaning of words. They should examine a dictionary in detail, so that they are able to make use of page headings and abbreviations.

Pupils should learn about:

The use of apostrophes to spell shortened forms,
e.gs. don't, they'd, we've

silent letters, as in 'gnat, know, pneumatic'

the relevance of roots and origins of words,
e.g. loveliness is to be found under lovely

the doubling of consonants, as in:

| tap — tapping | run — running |
| jab — jabbing | trip — tripping |

vowel deletion, as in:

| come — coming | hope — hoping |
| like — liking | cope — coping |

At all stages, children should be taught to proof-read their writing carefully to check for spelling errors.

PUPILS WITH WRITING AND SPELLING DIFFICULTIES SHOULD BE ENCOURAGED TO READ THEIR OWN WRITING ALOUD. IN THIS WAY, THEY CAN HEAR THE WORDS AS THEY SAY THEM. READING ALOUD ALSO HELPS THEM TO LISTEN FOR FULL STOPS AND COMMAS, I.E. TO IMPROVE PUNCTUATION.

The Importance of Correct Spelling in Examinations

On 25th July, 1991, the Secretary of State for Education stated that marks would be deducted for spelling, punctuation and grammar in each subject of the General Certificate of Secondary Education (GCSE). The arrangement began in 1992, the marks awarded for these skills being five per cent of the marks awarded for the specified writing skills in GCSE subjects. The regulations of the Joint Council for GCSE state as follows:

> 'It is not considered to be in the best interests of candidates to be exempted from this assessment but if exemption is requested and compensation, in the form of an adjustment to marks, is given there will be an indication on the certificate that special examination arrangements were made to enable the candidate to be assessed in the subject.'

No exemption from the assessment of spelling, punctuation and grammar is possible in English or in Welsh.

Arrangements for Scottish candidates are determined by the Scottish Examining Board.

Account of correct or incorrect spelling is taken at all Key Stages of the National Curriculum. For example, when the primary school pupil is asked to write a story, a letter and to learn to redraft his or her writing, accuracy of spelling has bearing on the level of performance awarded.

The Joint Council of GCSE issues a revised document in the autumn of each year. This is available to anyone on request. The current title:

'Guidance for Centres: Special arrangements and special consideration', is available from:

>> Joint Council for GCSE,
>> 6th Floor,
>> Netherton House,
>> 23/29 Marsh Street,
>> Bristol, BS1 4BP
>> Tel: (0272) 214379

Like handwriting, good spelling contributes to self respect and personal pride in written achievement. Self confidence is a likely contributor to examination success.

Some Things to Remember

1. *Always have a dictionary near your writing table.*

   Bookshops have a choice of larger print dictionaries that are easy to use. *An Easy Dictionary* by W.L. Darley, published by Schofield and Sims, is an easy one to begin with.

2. *Cut pieces of paper, 4 inches by 2 inches,* to use when you practise words. The word can be written at the top of the paper and folded over when you wish to *cover* or hide the word.

3. When you are learning to spell words, *try writing them with your eyes closed.* This will help you to *feel* how the words are formed, and will help you to learn more quickly. Later, you can write sentences with your eyes closed.

Some Questions and Answers

Q: *Why do some people find it difficult to spell correctly?*

A: In order to spell correctly you need to be able to:

   a) LOOK AT a word and remember what it looks like;
   b) LISTEN TO a word and remember what it sounds like;
   c) Put what you see with what you hear together in your memory;
   d) Write the word when you need to.

Q: *Are there different kinds of spelling problems?*

A: Yes.

Some people with difficulty cannot remember what words look like.

THEY HAVE POOR VISUAL MEMORIES.

Some people with difficulty cannot remember what words sound like.

THEY HAVE POOR AUDITORY MEMORIES.

Some people with difficulty cannot put together what they see with what they hear and then write the word on paper.

THEY HAVE POOR SOUND-TO-LETTER OR SYLLABLE MEMORIES.

Q: *Are there different ways of learning to spell?*

A: Yes, different problems need to be dealt with in different ways

Q: *How can I teach myself to spell?*

A: Try each method in turn, to find out which method suits you.

Visual Memory

Those with weak visual memories tend to write words as they sound, like this:

please	might be written as	plees
weather	might be written as	wether
night	might be written as	nite
field	might be written as	fyld

If you have a WEAK VISUAL MEMORY, try Spelling Method One.

Spelling Method One

1. Write the word correctly.
2. Look at the word, concentrating on the part you find most difficult.
3. Try to remember the word.
4. Cover up the word.
5. Write the word.
6. Check the word, by looking at the covered one.
7. Say the word.

Auditory Memory

Those with weak auditory memories tend to rely on remembering which letters are in words. They often get all or most of the letters correct, but they put them in the wrong order, like this:

should	might be written as	shloud or sholud
when	might be written as	wehn
night	might be written as	nihgt
table	might be written as	tbale

If you have a WEAK AUDITORY MEMORY, try Spelling Method Two.

Spelling Method Two

1. Write the word correctly.
2. Write the word again, naming each letter as you write it.
3. Say the word.
4. Try to remember the word.
5. Cover the word.
6. Write the word, naming each letter as you write it.
7. Check the word, by looking at the covered one.
8. Say the word.

You should also follow the syllables programme on pages 20-27.

Sound-to-Symbol Memory

Those with weak sound-to-letter or -syllable memories tend to write words in their own way. The words they write can sometimes be unrecognisable, like this:

television	might be written as	taviru
boat	might be written as	bto
table	might be written as	btel
cloth	might be written as	lcth

Students with this problem should:

a) relearn the alphabet, using letter names
b) relearn the letter sounds most commonly used for reading
c) practise writing each letter, so that they can be formed easily and correctly

If you have POOR SOUND-TO-LETTER OR -SYLLABLE MEMORY, try Spelling Method Three.

Spelling Method Three

1. Write the word correctly.
2. Say the word and find out how many beats (syllables) it has.
3. Look at the word, naming the letters as you look at them.
4. Cover the word.
5. Write the word, naming the letters as you write them.
6. Check the word by looking at the covered one.
7. Say the word.

Words You Will Need Most For Spelling and Writing

Of all the words you write as you improve your spelling, some are more important than others, because you will need them more often. For example, I am sure that you will understand that *a, and, the* and *is,* will all be used more often in your writing than words like *actually* and *helicopter.*

Often the most frequently written words are short ones such as *but, have, was* and *were.* Those words are often spelt incorrectly by poor spellers and stand out in written work, simply because they appear so often.

The words you need to write most often have been put together in a most interesting manner by the authors McNally and Murray. In *Figure 1,* they show which words are most often used in reading and writing, which are the next most frequently used words, and so on.

You have already looked at different ways of learning to spell words and have discovered which way works best for you. The best plan is to have *Figure 1* on your work table and learn one common word at a time, moving on to the next word as soon as you are ready. By choosing the most commonly used words for your spelling programme, you will become a good speller more quickly than choosing words that you will not often use. You will then have a special group of words to learn to spell.

Figure 1. Key Words to Literacy: A Proportional Representation of the most used words in English as applied to the vocabulary of an average adult.

12

a and he
I in is
it of that
the to was

all as at be but are for had have him his not on one said so they we with you 20

about an back been before big by call came can come could did do down first from get go has her here if into just like little look made make me more much must my no new now off only or our other out over right see she some their them then there this two when up want well went were what where which who will your old. 68

After Again Always Am Ask Another Any Away Bad Because Best Bird Black Blue Boy Bring Day Dog Don't Eat Every Fast Father Fell Find Five Fly Four Found Gave Girl Give Going Good Got Green Hand Head Help Home House How Jump Keep Know Last Left Let Live Long Man Many May Men Mother Mr. Never Next Once Open Own Play Put Ran Read Red Room Round Run Sat Saw Say School Should Sing Sit Soon Stop Take Tell Than These Thing Think Three Time Too Tree Under Us Very Walk White Why Wish Work Woman Would Yes Year Bus App'e Baby Bag Ball Bed Book Box Car Cat Children Cow Cup Dinner Doll Door Egg End Farm Fish Fun Hat Hill Horse Jam Letter Milk Money Morning Mrs. Name Night Nothing Picture Pig Place Rabbit Road Sea Shop Sister Street Sun Table Tea Today Top Toy Train Water 150

This area represents 19,750 further words. Space does not permit the printing of these words.

Points to Remember when Learning to Spell these Words

1. All words are not of equal value for improving spelling and writing.
2. Twelve words occur so frequently that they account for a quarter of the words we write.
3. About thirty words account for more than a third of the words we write.
4. About 100 words account for half the words we write.

   SO IT MAKES SENSE TO LEARN THESE WORDS

Your Key Word Spelling Record

Colour in the Key Word Numbers, one by one, when you are sure that you know how to spell them.

Figure 2.

Key Words Set One

1 a	21 have	41 came	61 made	81 some
2 and	22 him	42 can	62 make	82 their
3 he	23 his	43 come	63 me	83 them
4 I	24 not	44 could	64 more	84 then
5 in	23 on	45 did	65 much	85 there
6 is	26 one	46 do	66 must	86 this
7 it	27 said	47 down	67 my	87 two
8 of	28 so	48 first	68 no	88 when
9 that	29 they	49 from	69 new	89 up
10 the	40 we	50 get	70 now	90 want
11 to	31 with	51 go	71 off	91 well
12 was	32 you	52 has	72 only	92 went
13 all	33 about	53 her	73 or	93 were
14 as	34 an	54 here	74 our	94 what
15 at	35 back	55 if	75 other	95 where
16 be	36 been	56 into	76 out	96 which
17 but	37 before	57 just	77 over	97 who
18 are	38 big	58 like	78 right	98 will
19 for	39 by	59 little	79 see	99 your
20 had	40 call	60 look	80 she	100 old

WHEN YOU KNOW THESE WORDS, CHECK AND LEARN THE NEXT 150 KEY WORDS

Your Second Key Word Spelling Record

Colour in the Key Word Numbers, one by one, when you are sure that you know how to spell them.

Figure 3.

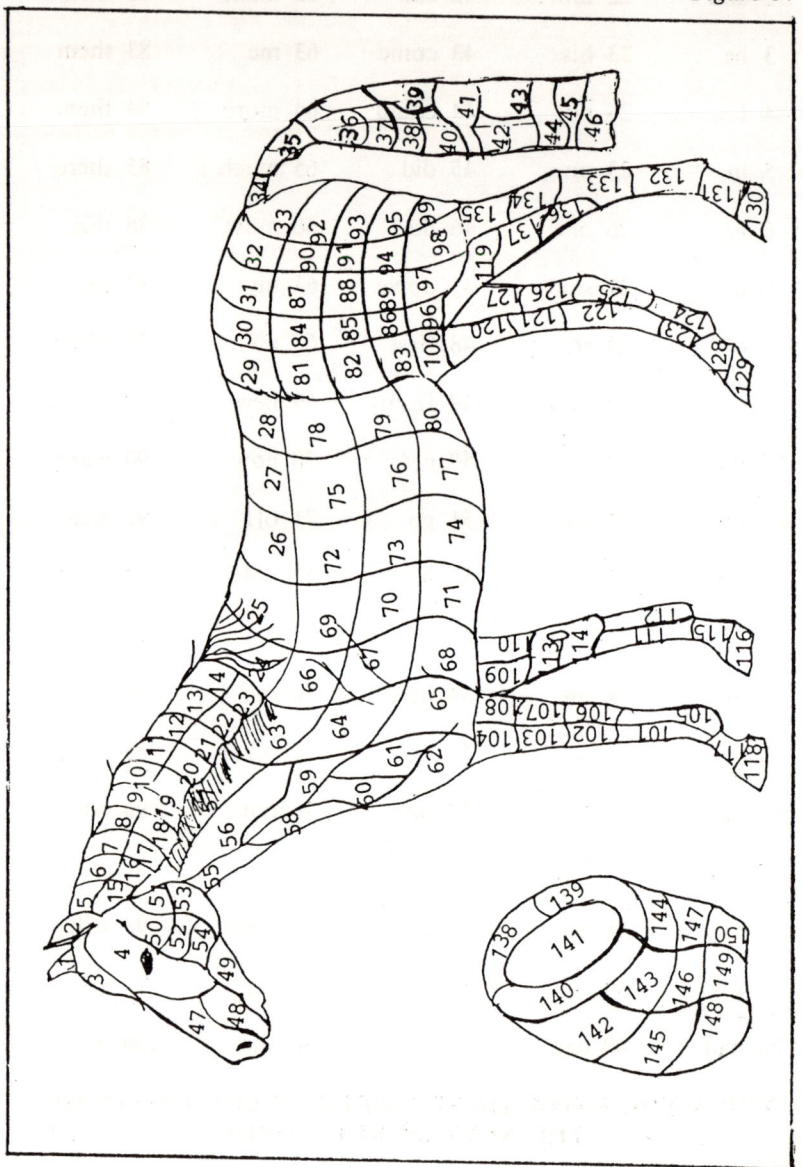

Key Words Set Two

1 after	31 girl	61 own	91 very	121 fun
2 again	32 give	62 play	92 walk	122 hat
3 always	33 going	63 put	93 white	123 hill
4 am	34 good	64 ran	94 why	124 horse
5 ask	35 got	65 read	95 wish	125 jam
6 another	36 green	66 red	96 work	126 letter
7 any	37 hand	67 room	97 woman	127 milk
8 away	38 head	68 round	98 would	128 money
9 bad	39 help	69 run	99 yes	129 morning
10 because	40 home	70 sat	100 year	130 Mrs.
11 best	41 house	71 saw	101 bus	131 name
12 bird	42 how	72 say	102 apple	132 night
13 black	43 jump	73 school	103 baby	133 nothing
14 blue	44 keep	74 should	104 bag	134 picture
15 boy	45 know	75 sing	105 ball	135 pig
16 bring	46 last	76 sit	106 bed	136 place
17 day	47 left	77 soon	107 book	137 rabbit
18 dog	48 let	78 stop	108 box	138 road
19 don't	49 live	79 take	109 car	139 sea
20 eat	50 long	80 tell	110 cat	140 shop
21 every	51 man	81 than	111 children	141 sister
22 fast	52 many	82 these	112 cow	142 street
23 father	53 may	83 thing	113 cup	143 sun
24 fell	54 men	84 think	114 dinner	144 table
25 find	55 mother	85 three	115 doll	145 tea
26 five	56 Mr.	86 time	116 door	146 today
27 fly	57 never	87 too	117 egg	147 top
28 four	58 next	88 tree	118 end	148 toy
29 found	59 once	89 under	119 farm	149 train
30 gave	60 open	90 us	120 fish	150 water

Letters and Syllables

Q: **what are the most important things to know about words?**

A: They are made up of letters and syllables.

1. They are made up of 26 letters of the alphabet.

2. Five very important letters of the alphabet are called vowels.
   All words have at least one vowel.
   The vowels are:

   a   e   i   o   u

   Make sure you know the names of the vowels and the sounds they most commonly make.

   When they are saying their names, vowels can be marked like this.

   ā   ē   ī   ō   ū

   When they are saying their easiest sounds, vowels can be marked like this:

   ă   ĕ   ĭ   ŏ   ŭ

3. The other 21 letters of the alphabet are called consonants.
   The consonants are:

   b c d f g h j k l m n p q r s t v w x y z

   Remember that *q* is always followed by *u:*   *QU* or *qu.*

Q: **What are syllables?**

A: Syllables are parts of words that we can hear as separate sounds. Try saying any word and find out how many beats it has. You can clap your hands or tap the table to find out about the beats or syllables in each word. For example:

	Syllables (Sound Beats)
cat dog big log:	1
insist playground garden cricket:	2
education delivery complication:	4

Closed Syllables
vowel-consonant (v.c.)

The first kind of syllable you will learn about is the *closed syllable.*

In a closed syllable, a consonant follows the vowel. The vowel says its short sound.

The vowel is shut in by the final consonant or consonants. This makes the vowel say its short sound.

These words have closed syllables. The mark for the short vowel sound is shown on each closed syllable.

căt bĭg măn whĕn sĕnt sprĭnt fŭnd fŏnt

Practise closed syllables

Read the words.

Write the words.

Mark the vowel as you say each word.

big	cat	cot	tap	pit	top	but	hut	met
set	shut	best	last	must	gets	fist	long	strong
fast	jump	limp	stamp	pest	just	bring	string	flint

Ask someone to dictate these sentences to you, one by one.

Write the sentences.

1. The big dog ran last, when he ran.
2. Can you jump into the big ring?
3. You must get strong this week.

Ask the person to dictate the sentences again. This time try writing them with your eyes closed.

Open Syllables
consonant-vowel or vowel (c.v.) or (v.)

The second kind of syllable you will learn about is the *open syllable*.

A syllable is open if one vowel is at the end. This vowel usually says its name. This is because there is no consonant at the end to close the vowel in.

The mark for the vowel sound is like this:

gō   bē   mē

Practise open syllables

Read the words.

Write the words.

Make a mark to separate the syllables, like this: **be/long**   **Es/so**

Mark the vowel in the open syllable as you say each world.

so	be	go	me	he	behave	lego
belong	Esso	hoping	hotel	moment	pupil	pilot

Ask someone to dictate these sentences to you, one by one.

Write the sentences.

1. So will the boy behave himself at the hotel?
2. The plane on the runway belongs to the pilot.

Ask the person to dictate the sentences again. This time try writing them with your eyes closed.

Vowel-Consonant-e Syllables
vowel-consonant-e (v.c.e.)

The third kind of syllable you will learn about is the vowel-consonant-e syllable.

A vowel-consonant-e syllable ends with an *e* that is silent.

The *e* at the end of the syllable makes the vowel before the consonant say its name.

This syllable is usually found at the end of a word.

The mark for the vowel sound is like this:

$\bar{a}$te   c$\bar{a}$me   f$\bar{i}$ne   t$\bar{u}$be   h$\bar{o}$me

Practise vowel-consonant-e syllables

Read the words.

Write the words.

The vowel-consonant-e syllable is at the end of each word. Mark the first vowel in the vowel-consonant-e syllable as you say each word.

| blame | came | tame | ozone | behave | pine | chime |
| tune | flute | explore | more | shore | jute | telephone |

Ask someone to dictate these sentences to you, one by one.

Write the sentences.
1. The man came to play a tune on his flute.
2. Can you blame the children when they do not behave?

Ask the person to dictate the sentences again. This time try writing them with your eyes closed.

Diphthong Syllables
vowel-vowel (v.v.)

The fourth kind of syllable you will learn about is the diphthong syllable.

In a diphthong syllable, the two vowels together make only one sound. The sound is most often the name of the first vowel, but sometimes the vowel says its common sound. The second vowel is silent.

The mark on the vowel sound is like this:

mēat	sēat	fēat	gōes	tōes	bōat
māin	rāin	sēen	flīes	brĕad	flūe

Practise diphthong syllables

Read the words.

Write the words.

Mark the first vowel in the diphthong syllables.

rain	plain	feet	seen	seat	moan	groan	been
green	blue	glue	sail	rail	mail	brain	train

Ask someone to dictate these sentences to you, one by one.

Write the sentences.
1. The man went out in the rain to sail his boat.
2. The mail train was late and the children were waiting for it.

Ask the person to dictate the sentences again. This time try writing them with your eyes closed.

Consonant-l-e Syllables

The fifth kind of syllable you will learn is the consonant-l-e syllable.

This syllable ends in an *e,* which is silent.

It comes at the end of a word.

With this syllable, the words end like this:

                ble   ple   zle   gle   tle   ple

Practise consonant-l-e syllables

Read the words.
Write the words.
Put a line under the consonant-l-e syllables.

table	fable	scrabble	marble	apple	dabble
topple	cripple	puzzle	muzzle	fizzle	embezzle

Ask someone to dictate these sentences to you.

Write the sentences.
1. The boy put the marble on the table.
2. The big apple began to topple from the tree.
3. The children wanted to play Scrabble.

Ask the person to dictate the sentences again. This time try writing them with your eyes closed.

Syllables with Vowel-r
vowel-r

The sixth syllable you will learn about is the vowel-r syllable. All vowels can be followed by *r* and the sounds they make are variable.

ar	er	ir	or	ur
arm	term	first	shorn	burn

Practise the vowel-r syllables

Read the words.

Write the words.

jar	farm	arm	star	warm	mark	term	her	germ
first	stir	squirt	birth	fur	curve	offer	suffer	buffer

Ask someone to dictate these sentences to you, one by one.

Write the sentences.
1. The girl had bare arms because it was such a warm night.
2. Did you offer the girl a fur coat to keep her warm in the dark?
3. The first train had no buffer so the men who were hurt began to suffer.

Ask the person to dictate the sentences again. This time try writing them with your eyes closed.

Now Practise the Syllables

Syllables are often, though not always, separated by two consonants.

Underline the vowels and diphthongs in the following words. Then separate the syllables.

The first four words have been done for you.

    scr<u>a</u>m/bl<u>e</u>   <u>in</u>/t<u>e</u>nd   sch<u>o</u>l/<u>ar</u>   t<u>a</u>/bl<u>e</u>

Now do the same with these words:

intend	extend	walkway	playground
gentleman	mummy	shelter	kennel
trumpet	falcon	convict	ladder
pastime	insist	invisible	microscope
person	cement	medical	doctor
table	garden	window	butter

Developing Spelling through Meaning

Mastery of the alphabet, Key Words, and syllable structure all assist with the teaching of spelling. However, all words have meanings, which have been derived from the languages that have shaped our own. For example, Greek, Latin, Old English, and French influences can be easily discerned in the words we use, and how each word is spelt will determine its meaning for us. The term 'morphology' refers to meaning, in this case to the meaning of words. Ramsden makes an excellent case for teaching spelling almost totally through meaning, showing that all our words have their origins and associations, and the way we spell can be traced back to them. Many words have root elements; the addition of a new part: prefix, suffix, or word ending, also determines or changes the word's meaning for us. An understanding of different word segments, helps the developing speller to become aware of word origins, to become sophisticated in the use of words and to manage written language in a mature manner.

Base elements are the same in words with related meanings. They can sometimes be base/root words. For example:

'sign' is the base element for:

> signature
> signal
> resign
> design

'ear' is the base element for:

> hear
> heard
> ear-ring

'you' is the base element for:

> your
> yours
> yourself

'burn' is the base element for:

> burned
> burning
> sunburn

(Ramsden, 1993, p.45)

A prefix occurs before the base/root word and affects meaning.

For example,

> the word 'born is changed by adding un — to make 'unborn'
> the word 'trust' is changed by adding mis — to make 'mistrust'

(Ramsden, 1993, pp.47-53)

Add prefixes to the following words:

> important
> happy
> take
> member
> tend

A suffix is added after the base/root word and affects meaning.

For example,

> the word 'king' is changed by adding dom — to make 'kingdom'
> the word 'brother' is changed by adding hood — to make 'brotherhood'

(Ramsden, 1993, pp.48-49)

Add suffixes to the following words:

> hope
> care
> know
> fellow
> other

Ramsden advises us to:

Segment words, using meaning as the first means of analysis, so that:

lovely	becomes	love - ly
wanting	becomes	want - ing
understand	becomes	under - stand

Understanding the term 'graph' allows the analysis:

photo para geo tele auto	graph	y ic al y er s

Understanding the term 'ward' allows the analysis:

to lee for a out	ward	ed ing ly s ing

Use the following base words to do your own word analyses and to build other words from the base word.

tend
port
table

A number of combinations from words and word parts allow us to spell correctly through segmenting and word meanings.

'Prefix — base word — suffix' is a common structure, so that 'unsightly' can be separated to its basic elements:

PREFIX	BASE WORD	SUFFIX
un	sight	ly

Practise finding parts of words that have meanings.

Divide the following words and put parts of each word under two or three columns:

	PREFIX	BASE WORD	SUFFIX
unhelpful			
management			
unsightly			
disenchanted			
understand			
pretend			

Now Test Yourself

Ask someone to read the words, one by one, so that you can write them from memory.

Test One

| are | said | they | about | before |
| call | could | first | new | other |

If you have spelt any words in Test One incorrectly, relearn all the *Key Words* on page 17.

Test Two

| after | always | because | every | found |
| head | know | many | should | nothing |

If you have spelt any words in Test Two incorrectly, relearn all the *Key Words* on page 19.

Test Three

| tap | but | met | shut | best |
| gets | strong | stamp | bring | flint |

If you have spelt any words in Test Three incorrectly, relearn the section on *closed syllables,* on page 21.

Test Four

| go | he | so | belong | hotel |
| hoping | moment | pupil | pilot | omit |

If you have spelt any words in Test Four incorrectly, relearn the section on *open syllables,* on page 22.

Test Five

ate	tame	ozone	behave	pine
chime	more	shore	jute	flute

If you have spelt any words in Test Five incorrectly, relearn the section on *vowel-consonant-e syllables,* on page 23.

Test Six

rain	feet	seat	moan	groan
blue	glue	sail	brain	train

If you have spelt any words in Test Six incorrectly, relearn the section on *dipthong syllables,* on page 24.

Test Seven

able	table	marble	apple	topple
cripple	puzzle	muzzle	fizzle	embezzle

If you have spelt any words in Test Seven incorrectly, relearn the section on *consonant-l-e syllables,* on page 25.

Test Eight

arm	star	warm	term	germ
first	birth	curve	offer	suffer

If you have spelt any words in Test Eight incorrectly, relearn the section on *vowel-r syllables,* on page 26.

Test Nine

design	unheard	dismember	fellowship	autograph
signature	portable	unsightly	pretended	disenchantment

If you have spelt any words in Test Nine incorrectly, relearn the section on **Spelling through Meaning**, on pages 28-31.

Some Useful Addresses

British Dyslexia Association, 98 London Road, Reading, RG1 5AU (0734 668271).
Centre for Left-Handed Studies/Left-Handed Company, PO Box 52, South DO, Manchester, M20 2PJ (061 445 0159).
Dyslexia Institute, 133 Gresham Road, Staines, Middlesex, TW18 2AJ (0784 463851). *Training in multi-sensory teaching techniques.*
Handwriting Interest Group, Secretary: Felicitie Barnes, 6 Fyfield Road, Ongar, Essex, CM5 0AH.
School Curriculum and Assessment Authority, Newcombe House, 45 Notting Hill Gate, London W11 3JB (071 229 1234).

Reference

Ramsden, M. Rescuing Spelling. Southgate, Crediton, 1993.

Dictionaries Suitable for Early Spellers

An Easy Dictionary, W.L. Darley, Schofield & Sims Ltd., Huddersfield, Revn. 1979.
Oxford Illustrated Junior Dictionary, R. Sansome & D. Reid, Oxford University Press, 1989.
Oxford Children's Dictionary, A. Spooner & J. Weston, Sphere Books, 1985.

Teachers who wish to know more about multi-sensory teaching of spelling should refer to:

The Hickey Multi-sensory Language Course, 2nd edition, eds. Jean Augur & Suzanne Briggs, Whurr Publishers Ltd., 19b Compton Terrace, London N1 2UN (071 359 5979).

Acknowledgement

Information about Key Words to Literacy and Figure 1, are printed by kind permission of William Murray, author of the following publications:

Key Words to Literacy and the Teaching of Reading, J. McNally & W. Murray, The Teacher Publishing Co., Kettering rev. 1968.
Key Words to Reading, M. Murray & J. Corby, Ladybird Books, Loughborough, 1991.

DEXTRAL BOOKS

PO Box 52, South D.O.,
Manchester M20 2PJ.
(Tel: 061 445 0159)

Educational books and resources
Handwriting and
left-handedness a speciality.

Sloping boards, pens, pencils,
pencil grips,
list of handwriting tutors.

We participate in exhibitions or
loan books for display.

THE LEFT-HANDED COMPANY
PO Box 52
South D.O.
Manchester
M20 2PJ

THE
LEFT HANDED
COMPANY

A unique mail order service
for left-handers

Scissors, rulers, pens, knives,
kitchen utensils and gifts

Suppliers to parents, schools,
special needs teachers, dyslexia,
language and learning, and
psychological services.

We participate in exhibitions and INSET days
or supply leaflets and display material.
Send 2nd class stamp for list of goods.

CLHS CENTRE FOR LEFT-HANDED STUDIES

The only Centre of its kind

for students researching sinistrality:
- bibliographies
- research papers
- books

media information service:
- interviews, features
- books for review

Helping left-handed children:
Illustrated lectures/workshops for:
schools, colleges, INSET and
parents' groups

Tel: 061 445 0159 for details.

Better Books & Software

(UK Distributors for Educators'
Publishing Service, USA.)

For the widest range in the UK of books on

SpLD (Dyslexia).

Please write or telephone for our list
of phonic reading schemes, reference
books, and other material relating to
special educational needs.

Organising a conference or exhibition?
We will be happy to bring along
our comprehensive display of
books for inspection and for sale.

3 Paganel Drive, DUDLEY, DY1 4AZ
Tel 0384 253276 Fax 0384 457979

 **p/t Post-graduate Diploma courses in Professional Studies in the Teaching of Students with SpLD/Dyslexia**

- offered by The Dyslexia Institute
- validated by Kingston University at 80 Masters level credits
- nationwide courses
- available to teachers and other relevant professionals
- courses cover: psychology and educational theory, teaching methods and practice in teaching
- The Dyslexia Institute Literacy Programme (DILP) in 2 volumes, is given as a course manual for those studying
- A first degree is not necessary

For further information please send large SAE to:
The Dyslexia Institute, 17 Station Road, Stone ST15 8JP.
Telephone: 0785 819497

HANDWRITING INTEREST GROUP

The Handwriting Interest Group has an active membership of 1,200. Its aims are to:

- raise standards in the teaching of handwriting in schools;
- disseminate teaching ideas and methods;
- develop assessment techniques and teaching programmes for pupils with handwriting difficulties;
- encourage and co-ordinate research.

Conferences, courses and workshops are arranged in many locations.

Handwriting Review, a journal with articles on teaching and assessment, and with usually more than 20 reviews, is published annually.

Membership Secretary: Felicitie Barnes
6 Fyfield Road, Ongar, Essex CM5 0AH.

Parent Booklet: *Handwriting . . . are you concerned* £2.00.
From: Beverly Scheib
1 D'Abernon Drive, Stoke D'Abernon, Surrey KT11 3JE.